GAS BOOK 08

BLUE SOURCE
CONTENTS

SHORT HISTORY
REPRESENTATIVE
IMAGE
PROJECT

PROJECT 01
CHEMICAL BROTHERS

PROJECT 02
**ADIDAS
PRESS CAMPAIGN**

PROJECT 03
COLDPLAY

PROJECT 04
FAULTLINE

PROJECT 05
ZAKEE SHARIFF

PROJECT 06
DIRTY VEGAS

PROJECT 07
TRAVIS

PROJECT 08
OTHERS

Q&A

BLUE SOURCE SHORT HISTORY

Blue Source are consistently nominated and awarded for major design awards year in and year out. Their video work has included films covering all sorts of musical genres. They are gaining an increasing reputation in the world of motion graphics, a title sequence for the quiz show, Banzai, won them a BAFTA award, one of the highest accolades in British broadcasting media. Their work is both popular with their contemporaries and the general public alike, yet it is interesting to examine the nature of their work and how their collaborations and relationships develop and have become intertwined within the creative process.

The offices of Blue Source are located in West London near the headquarters of Virgin Records. Their offices back onto the Grand Union Canal and just touch the shadow of Trellick tower, an impressive high-rise building constructed in the 1970s and designed by Erno Goldfinger. The offices, formerly belonging to an architectural practice, mean that the transition from one design function to another has changed the interior little. Yet the building is now reflective of their business, with editing suites on the ground floor and offices above. Most of the design work takes place around a central workstation with large format prints of previous successful projects overlooking newer work.

Leigh Marling and his wife Alison started the company in 1991 with Leigh's brother Seb joining soon after. Blue Source had existed, as a name, prior to this date where it was used to run a series of clubs as this was where Alison's background was and Leigh made his contribution as a DJ. This was the time of acid house where club culture was beginning to make a significant

dent in the popular consciousness. The origin of the name does not have a beginning but has many stories. One is that all popular music has its source in the Rhythm and Blues music of the United States. As their origin was in club culture, which its provenance firmly rooted in Black dance music, it seemed an appropriate title. To most of the founding members this is still apocryphal.

Leigh had the idea of setting up a design company having had some t-shirts designed to sell. Having no formal design education it was felt to be a positive move to create a company that could design club flyers and items needed to exist within this culture and offer it as a service to their friends and acquaintances. When Seb joined a more formal arrangement was undertaken with the setting up of an office in Wandsworth, South London. At this time they were looking for opportunities to establish their reputation. With a steady stream of flyer designs plus a friendship with Junior Boys Own there appeared to be more people they knew who were making records instead of playing them. From the very beginning it is very easy to detect a strand that is very important to them. That strand is collaboration. Having the intuition to be able to find the most appropriate person for whatever job is at hand has stayed with the company since this time and has woven itself into the fabric of the company.

What they regard as their first 'proper' sleeves were for the Stereo MC's and Leftfield, artwork, which made record companies sit up and take notice. For the record companies this was a successful record and had gone some way to commodifying a genre of music, which had been difficult to categorise and exploit.

Awareness of graphic design and its role in whatever process was always clearly understood but the actual process was being learnt as they went along. A mix of youthful enthusiasm and involvement in a culture under the world's style magnifying glass made for a design company that was unique in its outlook and in demand because of its position within this centre. The thought of leaving college and getting a production line graduate job was also an incentive for Seb in ensuring that Blue Source was to be a success.

The company began to galvanise its outlook. Design, at this point, was being wholly out sourced and it was not long before a studio had been established and designers were working there. As a design company the loose basis for any sort of model to compare with were Stylorouge, Michael Nash and Tomato. A group of people working together for common ends.

The move to West London was a turning point in the company realising the seriousness of Blue Source. 1993 saw Jonathon Cook and Borca Arleson, as designers, who brought a great deal of technical experience. Mark Tappin and Simon Earith have now replaced them.

Simon knew of their name, whilst at Middlesex School of Art, through the sleeves for Leftfield. Mark was in the year above him and was already working for Blue Source on a freelance basis. The defining factor was having his work spotted at his degree show in a gallery in Covent Garden, London. Following an informal interview he started work that afternoon. This was symptomatic of the terms of employment, at the time, with intuition being a major factor in whether

BLUE SOURCE OFFICE   PHOTO James Harris

REPRESENTATIVE IMAGE

a person was appropriate for the company. With a reputation to uphold Blue Source feel that they have to be more measured in the criteria they apply to the people who work there. This process is abetted by employing people on a freelance basis or as interns. Yet it is still personality driven and it is important never to move wholly away from how the company originally came into being. Further probing to divine exactly what this criteria is is a fruitless endeavour but it is safe to assume that a passion and a need to create excellent forms of visual communication is what drives the company presently, coupled with a desire to explore other areas.

The company do not aspire to have a house style but they are aware that people, external to the company, think that there is one. There is a sensibility in what they do in terms of process and quality of typography. It is also heavily ideas based, reliant on collaboration and instinctive. With music projects it is important to represent the music itself in a visual form, a medium that is abstract, in its bare components and is difficult to translate to another media effectively. The desire is to create a result that does not adhere to any tradition of creating sleeve artwork but alludes to another form of design, an art gallery exhibition catalogue, for instance. Working at that conceptual and abstract level has been an enormous bonus in garnering other commissions away from the industry. The ideas are generally perceived as non-specific to the medium they are finalised in which makes it easier when they work in other areas because they are not generic to one form of media. To be ghettoised in one form of design and to create ideas for that one form can be very restraining. It is part of a need to not think about the end result, and look to the other

areas that stimulates their output and retains the vigour in their work.

The subject of collaboration is multi-faceted. It is a combination of personal friendship, appropriateness for the project at hand and a personal regard for their work. These factors are interchangeable and have different levels of emphasis. There are a number of people whose work they are being constantly exposed to but are awaiting for an appropriate project to present itself but they have a very astute knowledge of when their work will be put to good use. It is important to establish a dialogue, in the first instance, and not just to call people in when a project needs to be resourced. This further develops into a deeper friendship where there is no longer the need for discourse on a business level. The period between seeing someone's work and actually using him or her can turn into a period of years. It is a constant quest to be aware of everything that is currently available and establishing a bank of information and has bound itself into the daily function of the company. Inversely they can have an idea that cannot have an immediately apparent source of imagery and the quest for collaborators takes on a different set of criteria with the project being built up from nothing, without any structure being in place. The level of direction given to the collaborator varies but is given greater weight to photographers. The design process for Blue Source is wholly motivated by a faith in the concept that needs to be produced and this affects how the project is produced with the collaborator acting as facilitator to the one idea. Whoever is commissioned becomes temporarily part of the Blue Source process.

Ideas generation, the collaboration and close relationships are indelible elements of a Blue Source project. This is what is representative of what could be defined as the Blue Source philosophy, a philosophy that none of the protagonists would subscribe fully to but are linked by in varying degrees.

A long-standing relationship with The Chemical Brothers and the photographer, Jonathon de Villiers conspired to create this image. It was to be used to adorn the cover of a compilation called The Brothers Gonna Work It Out. At the outset of the project there were no parameters in place that would dictate the outcome. The result is regarded as representative of a balance between all the elements listed above. The image signifies hope, is loaded with irony, is technically perfect and is also not what would be expected of a dance music compilation cover. Blue Source read a religious overtone into the title, hence an image of a church and a further subversion is acted out on the viewer by selecting a church which looks distinctly like it is in middle America when in fact, it is in Harlow in Middlesex, an urban sprawl on the edge of London. There has been no image manipulation; even the sign was constructed by Blue Source and erected outside the church in time to catch worshippers leaving after a Sunday morning service.

1

1

IMAGE FROM CHEMICAL BROTHERS "BROTHERS GONNA WORK IT OUT"

PROJECT 01 CHEMICAL BROTHERS

Out of any music produced currently the Chemical Brothers have a very distinct style to their image which have been significantly bolstered by the work of Kate Gibb with art-direction and design by Mark Tappin at Blue Source. They attempted to create the visual style of the band digitally but the results had been too cold. It was only when they saw her work that the collaboration was pulled into focus.

The band have been totally happy with this working relationship that had been created with the previous album, Surrender, and were looking to capitalise what had become a pleasurable experience for everyone involved. There was a desire to keep a similar feel to the artwork but it was felt that it needed to be shifted slightly in newer directions to make it more marketable and for it to exist and appeal to people beyond the boundaries of the co-collaborators and die hard fans.

This allowed Blue Source the freedom to be experimental with the image making process and the chance to develop their creative relationship with Kate Gibb. The process took the form of sourcing images from picture libraries which was

undertaken together and reaped a quantity of 50 to 100 images. All of these images were presented to the band to see if there were figures, shapes, textures or objects which would sit within the direction of the music and their ideas. The short list was then taken away and a series of artworks was prepared from this distilled information. At interval stages the band would be invited to view the work in progress and select what was suitable for what release.

As part of that process the promo sleeves provided the templates for the pieces that Kate would screen print for the final commercial sleeve artwork. The promo sleeves acted as the visuals that the band would be shown and act as aids in the presentation and approval process. Anywhere between three or five versions of any image would be created by Kate for the band to select from.

The process has created multi-layered results which can only be realised through an organic creative process, something which is unique to this group, art direction and design company plus image maker.

There is a reticence to use the phrase retro to

describe Kate Gibb's work but this feeling is driven by the Chemical Brothers who are enormous personal fans of her work. At the same time it has a modernity to it which is akin to a perception of the future which may have been relevant in times past.

The band's logo has been retained since their first album and is not the work of Blue Source. Once again it is an element that the band have kept but they like it.
Like Kate Gibb's work even the logo has taken on a life of its own and is very popular with their fan base.

The direction it could be taken is limitless and potentially experimental. An indication of what could happen was a television commercial to promote the album. It was intentionally commissioned after they had been presented with final artwork for the sleeve. Mark Tappin created the commercial, in house at Blue Source. Mark plays a cameo role in the commercial. The commercial ties in with the sleeve artwork but a storyboard and treatment were created framed with images from the album campaign interspersed with ideas about the animation as a sequence.

1

CHEMICAL BROTHERS "COME WITH US" / CD Album (Front)   Virgin Records   2002   Art Direction, Design: Mark Tappin
Cover Art: Kate Gibb

01 # COME WITH US
02 # IT BEGAN IN AFRIKA
03 # GALAXY BOUNCE
04 # STAR GUITAR
05 # HOOPS
06 # MY ELASTIC EYE
07 # THE STATE WE'RE IN
08 # DENMARK
09 # PIONEER SKIES
10 # THE TEST

  Virgin Freestyle Dust

7 24381 16822 6

| 1 | | | CHEMICAL BROTHERS "COME WITH US" / CD Album (Reverse) | Virgin Records | 2002 | Art Direction, Design: Mark Tappin Cover Art: Kate Gibb |
| 2 | 1 | 2 | CHEMICAL BROTHERS "COME WITH US" / CD Album (Booklet Spread) | Virgin Records | 2002 | Art Direction, Design: Mark Tappin Cover Art: Kate Gibb |

All songs written by Rowlands/Simons
The Players – Tom Rowlands and Ed Simons
The Producers – The Chemical Brothers
The Engineer – Steve Dub
The Assistant – Greg Fleming

Vocals – Beth Orton and Richard Ashcroft
Additional Musicians – Stowell, Beverley Skeete, Greg Fleming

Recorded at Milton Studios, South London
Edited by Cheeky Paul in the basement
Mastered by Mike Marsh at The Exchange
Art Direction by Blue Source and The Chemical Brothers
Art Screenprints by Kate Gibb

Thanks to Robert, Nick and Clare at MBL, Steve Brown,
Keith Wood, Errol, Glenn and Ali at Astralwerks, everyone at
Virgin Records and all at XL

Beth Orton appears courtesy of Heavenly Recordings.
Richard Ashcroft appears courtesy of Hut Recordings.

01 'Come With Us' co-written by Rallo/Gropper/ash/Kelsen
'Fairwins contains a sample from the recording 'The Evidence'
licensed courtesy of G. Chenrussy and J. Claudel. 02 'It Began
In Afrika' co-written by Ingram contains a sample from
'Drumbeat' performed by Jim Ingram, courtesy of Star
Records/Fantasy Inc. 03 'Hoops' co-written by Alexander
features samples from The Association recording 'Round Again'
(Alexander). Produced under license from Warner Bros.
Records. By arrangement with Warner Special Projects.
06 'My Elastic Eye' co-written by Esterely contains elements
sampled from 'Tic Toc Sentizena' (Esterely), Tele Music
Records (1973). Used by permission. All rights reserved.
9 'Pioneer Skies' co-written by Caralson/Bachelet contains
elements sampled from 'Yellow Train' (Jamison/Bachelet),
'Treeco Records (1973. Used by permission. All rights
reserved. 10 'The Test' co-written by Guslaw Niemen
contains part of the improvisation performed by C. Niemen
for the recording 'Telegrym', originally released on the LP
'Niemen Aerolit' (1976, catalogue number SX 1391, by Polskie
Nagrania Muza.

All tracks published by Universal/MCA Music Limited except
0102 published by Universal/MCA Music Limited/Copyright
Control, 06 published by Universal/MCA Music
Limited/Ardmore & Beechwood Ltd, 0910 published by
Universal/MCA Music Limited/Universal Music and
Abaco/ash/BMG Music Publishing Ltd and 10 published in
Universal/MCA Music Limited/EMI Music Publishing
Ltd/P&A. ℗ & © 2002 Virgin Records Limited. This label copy
is the subject of copyright protection. All rights reserved
by Virgin Records Limited. The copyright in this sound
recording is owned by Virgin Records Limited.
7243 8 11682 2 6 XDUSE

STAR GUITAR

1			CHEMICAL BROTHERS "STAR GUITAR" / Vinyl Single (Front)	Virgin Records	2002	Art Direction, Design: Mark Tappin Cover Art: Kate Gibb
2	1	2	CHEMICAL BROTHERS "STAR GUITAR" / Vinyl Single (Reverse)	Virgin Records	2002	Art Direction, Design: Mark Tappin Cover Art: Kate Gibb

A **STAR GUITAR**

B **STAR GUITAR PETE HELLER'S EXPANDED MIX**

All tracks written by Rowlands/Simons and produced by The Chemical
Brothers. Track A edited by Cheeky Paul. Engineered by Steve Dub.
Track B remix and additional production by Pete Heller for Junior
Productions. Remix engineer Gary Wilkinson. All tracks additional vocals by
Beverley Skeete. All tracks published by Universal/MCA Music Limited.
Art Direction Blue Source and The Chemical Brothers. Art Screenprints by
Kate Gibb. ℗ & © 2001 Virgin Records Limited. This label copy is the subject
of copyright protection. All rights reserved. © 2001 Virgin Records Limited.
The copyright in this sound recording is owned by Virgin Records Limited.
Printed in the E.U. LC03098/PM514/7243 5 46169 6 9/CHEMST14.

7 24381 16822 6

| 1 | | | CHEMICAL BROTHERS "COME WITH US" / CD Single (Front) | Virgin Records | 2002 | Art Direction, Design: Mark Tappin
Cover Art: Kate Gibb |
| 2 | 1 | 2 | CHEMICAL BROTHERS "COME WITH US" / CD Single (Reverse) | Virgin Records | 2002 | Art Direction, Design: Mark Tappin
Cover Art: Kate Gibb |

01

COME WITH US—EDIT

02

H.I.A

03

COME WITH US FATBOY SLIM REMIX

All tracks written by Rowlands/Simons except 01&03 co-written by Cooperman/Krissen/Fairstein. Track 02 co-written by Heard/Owens. All tracks produced by The Chemical Brothers. All tracks engineered by Steve Dub. 03 Remix by Fatboy Slim. Mixed and Engineerd by Simon Thornton. All tracks mastered at The Exchange. Tracks 01/03 contain a sample from the recording 'The Evidence' licensed courtesy of G. Chemouny and J. Claudel. 02 contains elements from 'Music Take Me Up' (L Heard, R. Owens) by Fingers Inc. Published by Westbury Music Ltd/Musical Directions (MCPS)/Alleviated Music (ASCAP), used by permission. All rights reserved. 01/03 Published by Universal/MCA Music Limited/Copyright Control. 02 published by Universal/MCA Music Limted/Alleviated Music(ASCAP)/Westbury Music Ltd/Musical Direction (MCPS). ℗ & © 2002 Virgin Records Limited. This label copy is the subject of copyright protection. All rights reserved. © 2002 Virgin Records Limited. The copyright in this sound recording is owned by Virgin Records Ltd. Printed in the E.U. Art Direction Blue Source and The Chemical Brothers. Art Screenprints by Kate Gibb. LC03098/PM514/7243 5 46355 2 6/CHEMSD15.

Brothers Gonna Work It Out

1			CHEMICAL BROTHERS "BROTHERS GONNA WORK IT OUT" / Mix CD (CD Sleeve)	Virgin Records	1998	Art Direction, Design: Mark Tappin Cover Photo: Jonathon De Villiers
2	1	2	CHEMICAL BROTHERS "BROTHERS GONNA WORK IT OUT" / Mix CD (Front And Back Cover)	Virgin Records	1998	Art Direction, Design: Mark Tappin Cover Photo: Jonathon De Villiers
3		3	CHEMICAL BROTHERS "BROTHERS GONNA WORK IT OUT" / Mix CD (Inner Catefold)	Virgin Records	1998	Art Direction, Design: Mark Tappin Cover Photo: Jonathon De Villiers

BROTHER'S GONNA WORK IT OUT A DJ MIX ALBUM BY THE CHEMICAL BROTHERS

1. 01 WILLIE HUTCH. BROTHER'S GONNA WORK IT OUT 02 CHEMICAL BROTHERS WITH JUSTIN WARFIELD. NOT ANOTHER DRUGSTORE – PLANET NINE MIX 03 CHEMICAL BROTHERS. BLOCK ROCKIN' BEATS – THE MICRONAUTS MIX 04 ON THE HOUSE. THIS AIN'T CHICAGO 05 THE JIMMY CASTOR BUNCH. IT'S JUST BEGUN **2.** 06 KENNY DOPE PRESENTS THE POWERHOUSE THREE. MAKIN' A LIVING 07 BADDER THAN EVIL. HOT WHEELS – THE CHASE 08 UNIQUE 3 THE THEME – UNIQUE MIX 09 LOVE CORPORATION. GIMME SOME LOVE **3.** 10 THE MICRONAUTS. THE JAZZ 11 THE SEROTONIN PROJECT. SIDEWINDER – 312 VS 216 STOMP MIX 12 CARLOS 'AFTER DARK' BERRIOS. DOIN' IT AFTER DARK (D-SKI'S DANCE) 13 FREESTYLE. DON'T STOP THE ROCK 14 METRO L.A. TO A NATION ROCKIN' **4.** 15 CHEMICAL BROTHERS. MORNING LEMON 16 MEAT BEAT MANIFESTO. MARS NEEDS WOMEN 17 RENEGADE SOUNDWAVE. THUNDER 18 DBX. LOSING CONTROL 19 DUBTRIBE SOUND SYSTEM. MOTHER EARTH **5.** 20 BARRY DE VORZON AND PERRY BOTKIN JNR. THE RIOT 21 THE ULTRAVIOLET CATASTROPHE. TRIP HARDER 22 MANIC STREET PREACHERS. EVERYTHING MUST GO – CHEMICAL BROTHERS REMIX 23 SPIRITUALIZED. I THINK I'M IN LOVE – CHEMICAL BROTHERS VOCAL REMIX

XDUSTCD101/7243 846090 24, LC 3098, PM 528. PRINTED IN THE EU

 the chemical brothers | Freestyle Dust | Virgin

BROTHER'S GONNA WORK IT OUT A DJ MIX ALBUM BY THE CHEMICAL BROTHERS XDUSTCD101/7243 846090 24

Brothers Gonna Work It Out

Take This Brother May It Serve You Well

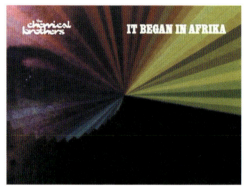

1   CHEMICAL BROTHERS "COME WITH US" / TV Advert   Virgin Records   2002   Art Direction: Mark Tappin
    Design: Terry Lewis

1   CHEMICAL BROTHERS "COME WITH US" / TV Advert   Virgin Records   2002   Art Direction: Mark Tappin
    Design: Terry Lewis

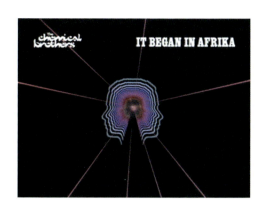

PROJECT 02 ADIDAS PRESS CAMPAIGN

Blue Source was approached to represent, visually, new adidas footwear technologies that had been developed. adidas wanted, in some way, to exploit a visual style that they had seen in their previous work and move the way their footwear was realised up to that point which had been very product shot based advertising. This press campaign was to run alongside more major advertising campaigns allowing Blue Source to be a bit more artistic and abstract with these representations and what this technology could look like. The new range in development was called adidas A3 and through collaboration with selected image-makers the process of articulation could begin.

A two to three month research period was undertaken into shoe technology and the more traditional methods of describing movement. This was based in the scientific and biological and this data had to be fed into a style-oriented template. Each image was to play on one aspect of what a shoe does.

A concept image was created in house creating a prototype or template to show other people who were to collaborate on the project and give them an indication of the direction that Blue Source were directing. The brief, when written or spoken, was found to be too abstract to explain so this initial image was very useful. It also provided a working model for the client to ensure that the project was moving in the right direction.

The collaboration was between three groups or individuals; Kam Tang, Lost in Space, who produced a short animation sequence fully describing movement. The third person was James Dimmock, a photographer. All three individuals seemed to be producing the style and language of work that was required for the campaign. The process of creation was not only showing them the concept image that Blue Source had created but a lengthy period of dialogue and collaboration with plenty of healthy debate about what was required, especially as Blue Source had spent a great deal of time in research into the project. A two-week period was allotted to delivering final artwork for what was, at times, a fraught but ultimately rewarding assignment.

1

ADIDAS TENET II / Campaign Art Work   Adidas   2001   Art Direction: Leigh Marling & Mark Tappin
Design: Mark Tappin
Art: Lost In Space

adidas
FOREVER SPORT

02.1   02.2

adidas Tenet II
Foot Wrapping Technology
Animation by Lost In Space

1				ADIDAS TECHNOLOGIES / Concept Art Work	Adidas	2001	Art Direction: Leigh Marling & Mark Tappin Design: Mark Tappin Art: Mark Tappin
	1	2					
2				ADIDAS WATER MOCCASIN / Campaign Art Work	Adidas	2001	Art Direction: Leigh Marling & Mark Tappin Design: Mark Tappin Art: James Dimmock

03.1   03.2

adidas Water Moccasin
Outsole Grip Technology
Image created by James Dimmock

adidas
FOREVER SPORT

adidas®
FOREVER SPORT

1			ADIDAS STAR RACER / Campaign Art Work	Adidas	2001	Art Direction: Leigh Marling & Mark Tappin
	1					Design: Mark Tappin
						Art: Kam Tang

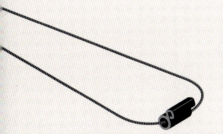

01.1   01.2

adidas Star Racer
Exoskeleton Lacing Technology
Illustration by Kam Tang

PROJECT 03 COLDPLAY

Following the international success of their first album, Coldplay approached Blue Source for their second release. The first album had been put together with considerable urgency and this project gives them a greater opportunity to contemplate the direction it will take. Based on a proven track record the band gave them a verbal brief in which they were keen to produce a set of images for the sleeves that depicted images of the band themselves in a non-typical fashion and those images to be more graphic but still represent them individually in some way. Images that had a grace to them, were resonant of drawing as medium and were contemporary in feel. The task was to find a balance between these differing needs and, after further discussions, the work of fashion photographer Sølve Sunsbø.

Sølve was an image maker that Blue Source had been keen to work with for some time but had not found an appropriate project for this to happen. His work had been considered as part of the research for the adidas press campaign and his style best suited the differing needs of the Coldplay release. The style of work Blue Source were after had been a language Sølve has been developing and provided an opportunity to take advantage of his knowledge and understanding of this particular image production. Each release will feature a photograph of a band member, as a portrait.

They vary from the outline of the face being very legible to being far more abstract with the viewer unsure of the angle or the proximity to the image itself. To the band it had a life-drawing and sculptural aspect to it but had been rendered digitally. The end result is a wire frame-type model with the opportunity of the image-maker being able to determine how legible the image will be.

1

COLDPLAY "IN MY PLACE" / CD Single (Front)　　　　　EMI Records　　　　2002　　　　Art Direction, Design: Mark Tappin
　　　Cover Art: Sølve Sundsbø

COLDPLAY IN MY PLACE

COLDPLAY A RUSH OF BLOOD TO THE HEAD

1

1

COLDPLAY "A RUSH OF BLOOD TO THE HEAD" / CD Album (Front)   EMI Records   2002   Design: Mark Tappin
                                                                                                          Cover Art: Sølve Sundsbø

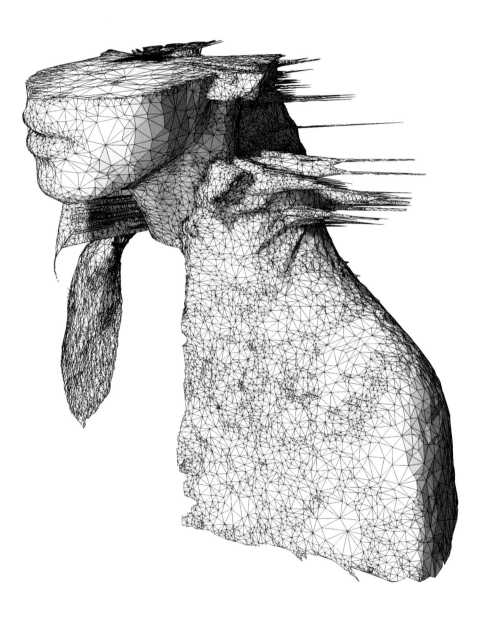

PROJECT 04
FAULTLINE

This is the second release for this music project founded by David Kosten. The music is a mix of the electronic book ended with an abrasiveness, at one extreme, and the melodic at the other. Once again there was a great deal of awareness of the work of Blue Source prior to commencement of the project. David Kosten had a very clear idea of how he wished to be presented though not seeing himself as particularly visually minded but was taking his cues from the music he was creating to tell him when the visual idea had been achieved.

The idea was to create images that distilled qualities found in the music itself, the abrasiveness and the melodiousness. It was felt that using everyday objects and rendering them functionless, in some way, could best exemplify this. This idea was amplified through the method of how these selected objects were rendered. One of the original ideas around this theme was

make the objects seen petrified, like the artefacts unearthed at Pompeii, after Mount Vesuvius had erupted in Roman times. The surface detail of the objects had been removed but the form would remain creating a familiar object but celebrating its beauty.

The selection of the objects is based on them being familiar and domestic but principally for their form. Tim Magdalino who cast the objects in resin at life size did the modelling. Blue Source selected the objects used and discussed them with David, though it was clearly apparent that certain objects were more preferable than others during this selection process. Merton Gauster took the photographs and is regarded as their photographer of choice with this type of project. The objects were photographed on glass and composited onto a photographic graduated background. The plug socket was found in the Blue Source producer's

mother in-laws house. The remote control is the companies own with the camera being found in a cheap tourist shop. The wrench had to be specially ordered from Scandinavia. The only object that was hired was the razor. David Kosten was most keen for the wrench to be the sleeve image.

Another facet of the objects is that they have all been superseded by subsequent technologies or improvements to their design or function adding a patina of things trapped in time.

The typography was deliberately selected for its functional and documentary aesthetic giving a feeling that these objects had been photographed and catalogued. The idea was to make the type appear under designed and functional. The only labelling on the front of the album was a removable catalogue number label.

1

	1

FAULTLINE "YOUR LOVE MEANS EVERYTHING" / CD Album   Blanco Y Negro   2002   Art Direction,Design: Simon Earith
Cover Art: Simon Earith, Tim Magdalino
Photo: Merton Gauster

| 1 | | | FAULTLINE "YOUR LOVE MEANS EVERYTHING" / CD Album | Blanco Y Negro | 2002 | Art Direction,Design: Simon Earith
Cover Art: Simon Earith, Tim Magdalino
Photo: Merton Gauster |
| 2 | 1 | 2 | FAULTLINE "YOUR LOVE MEANS EVERYTHING" / CD Album | Blanco Y Negro | 2002 | Art Direction,Design: Simon Earith
Cover Art: Simon Earith, Tim Magdalino
Photo: Merton Gauster |

PROJECT 05
ZAKEE SHARIFF

Zakee Shariff is London based fashion label. Zakee Shariff herself is the designer at the helm and having trained in fine art printed textiles practices in a way that questions and stretches the possibilities of traditional label output beyond the production of key clothing ranges.

For example Zakee does not show her collections on the catwalk but prefers to create a seasonal presentation in key cities. In the past, these presentations have resulted in film screenings and exhibitions. The Autumn/Winter 2003 London presentation saw Zakee Shariff print across large format black and white fine art photography and invite a number of people present to wear the clothes from the forthcoming collection to the opening event. Similarly to Blue Source her practice is often very collaborative.

Blue Source had known Zakee socially for a number of years and was asked to update an existing identity as part of her need to draw

together the strands of her business and create a new identity. Blue Source saw this as an opportunity to stretch their work into the areas of fashion and corporate identity, sectors away from the music industry, and Zakee was fortunate to benefit from their input for little or no design fee. They also have a great deal of empathy with her work believing it to be very accessible, a factor that is important in their other work. Zakee, as a client, was very open to any input but is very certain about the message her clothes are meant to convey, as message that states that you do not have to be one type of person to wear her garments.

The solution was arrived through what Blue Source see as a refining process, moving ever closer to what they saw her clothing as bearing in mind what her company was perceived as and not transforming it into some kind of ultra-slick proposition. It was important

to retain the values of craft, process and idiosyncrasy of her clothes and not to create the idea of a global high fashion super brand. The continuity between the old identity and the new was the White on White effect of her labelling continuing onto her swing tags.

The closeness of the relationship has grown into role for Blue Source as label art direction and design consultants, which has translated into designs for swing tag & neck labels, an identity for Shariff's diffusion range called Maggie, working as an accompaniment to the core range. There will be mens wear range called folk where the design ideas will be motivated by the stitching processes in neck labels.

The logo was hand drawn and was one of five options that were presented which were then refined further using different elements from different ideas and amalgamating them into one identity.

ZAKEE SHARIFF

ZAKEE SHARIFF / Identity   Zakee Shariff   2002   Art Direction, Design: Simon Earith

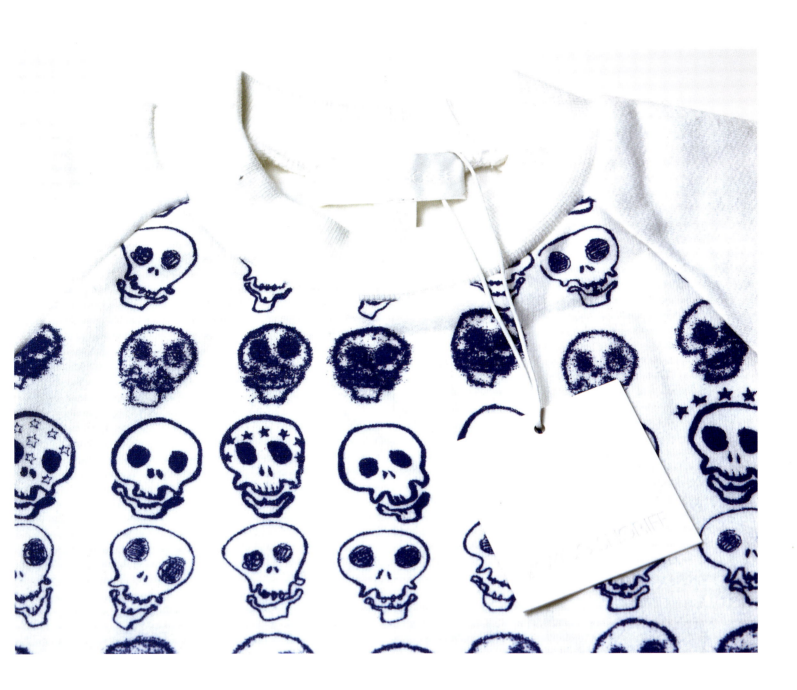

PROJECT 06
DIRTY VEGAS

Dirty Vegas are a group signed to Parlophone Records. Their music straddles two genres, traditional song writing on the one hand and the production values associated with club music on the other. The motivation to work with Blue Source came from the bands manager, Dave Dorrell, who approached the company 12 months prior to commencement of work on the campaign. He was after a creative solution that would be adaptable for a longer media campaign, encompassing an album and a number of singles. Both Blue Source and Dave Dorrell had been aware of each other's work for a number of years, both parties origins being based within dance music culture. The process of arriving at the ideas was completed independent of the bands involvement initially, evolving within the 12 months the first single cover being based on a Japanese illustration. This was to be the basis for the style of the whole campaign but this

was to change direction, principally because the musical content of this single was so far way from the rest of their music. This was coupled with the need to create a stylistic direction with a more international flavour to it, tying in cues from American culture into the artwork. This was not done for reasons of business but to create an air of mystery by not tying the band to any national identity.

This new motivation commenced with research into signage as the source of images with other ideas based on fantasy illustration and through this process they came across the paintings of Richard Phillips and presented the possibility of featuring his work to the band. Painterly hyperrealism seems to characterise his style, incorporating material taken from a range of cultural sources such as pornography, advertising and fashion spreads. The work

focuses mainly on women in close up mimicking the style of glamour photography with its readily available sexual message. It also has links to the type of imagery that modern club culture utilises to promote itself in a very clichèd sense coupled with a strip show aesthetic. The paintings featured in the campaign were done so with the kind permission of the artist and Friedrich Petzel Gallery, New York. Richard Phillips collaborated with Blue Source by supplying a selection of his work for possible inclusion in the campaign, from which six images were short-listed for the project.

The logo for the group was being developed in parallel with the image research with a subtle reference to 1970's Las Vegas-type signage. The typeface, Dynamo, was not specially drawn but found in an old Letraset catalogue and had to be sourced from a type foundry.

1		
		1

<u>DIRTY VEGAS</u> / CD Album (Front)   Parlophone Records   2002   Art Direction, Design: Simon Earith
(US / UK)   Cover Art: Richard Phillips

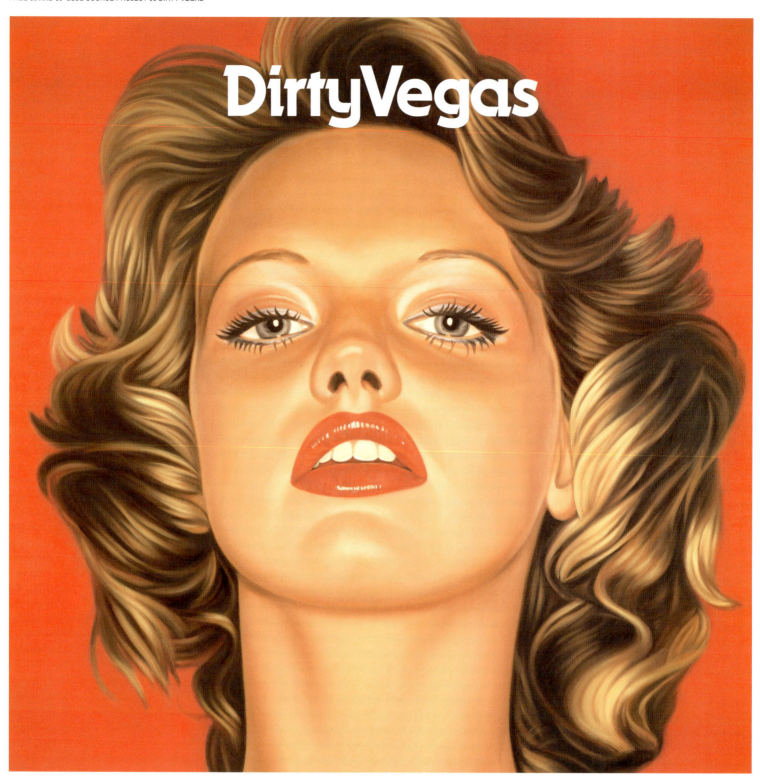

1			DIRTY VEGAS / GHOSTS CD Single (Front)	Parlophone Records (US / UK)	2002	Art Direction, Design: Simon Earith Cover Art: Richard Phillips
2	1	2	DIRTY VEGAS / DAYS GO BY CD Single (Front)	Parlophone Records (US / UK)	2002	Art Direction, Design: Simon Earith Cover Art: Richard Phillips

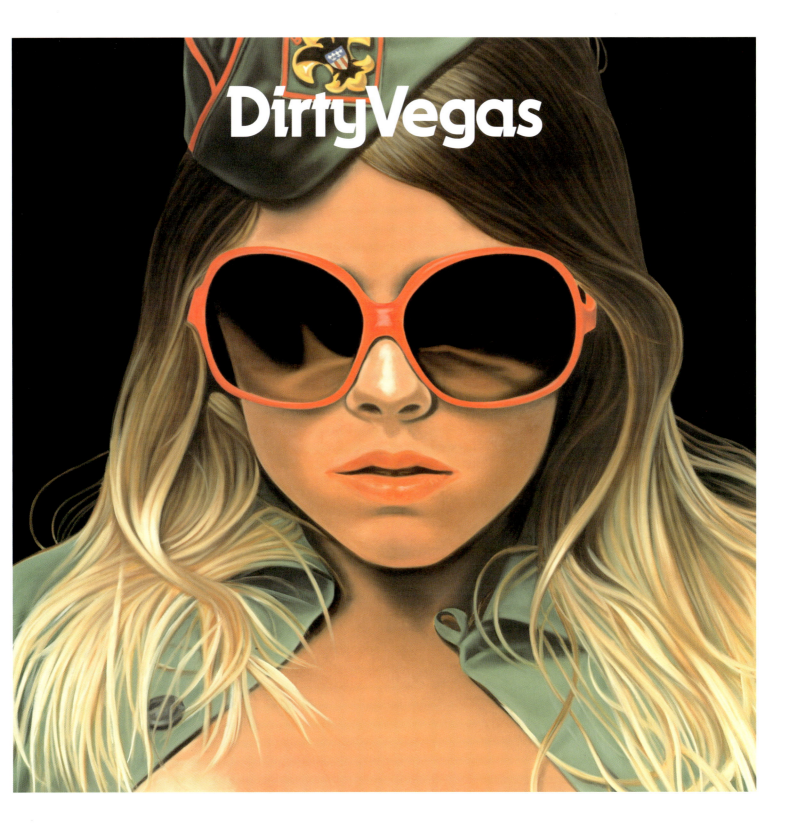

PROJECT 07
TRAVIS

The group and the record company initiated the EP More Than Us. The group had a relationship with an existing designer but their work for Caterpillar was the galvanising factor at the start of this project. The EP's are classed as side projects coming, as they do, between major album and single releases and the desire was to resource these releases with the use of Blue Source plus a photographer.

The idea pertains to the title in some way. The deliberate choice of a factory made moulded chair, in a number of configurations pertained to the idea of a collection of people, without seeing individuals, particularly the image of four chairs lined up behind a desk. Bridget Smith, whose work they were familiar with, took the pictures. Her shots of landscapes and domestic interiors had been seen in the contemporary art magazine Frieze along with her work being exhibited in a London gallery. The spaces are very antiseptic

and have no link to music and the band nominated this space because it had a graphic quality to it.

The second EP, Coming Around, utilised the photographic work of artist Bridget Smith, once again, continued the theme of de-populated interiors and chairs. The emptiness would be filled later on album and single artwork allowing the EP to serve as a negative space, visually. The image for this EP was shot in Japan, as opposed to an office space in the Truman Brewery in London for More Than Us, following various emails to Bridget when she was there working on an unrelated project. Because the group were happy with the first EP they were happy for Bridget to continue to shoot to develop the campaign.

The singles from the album The Invisible Band drew on the paintings of the American artist

Andrew Wyeth in terms of their colour, composition, mood and relationship to the music. There was a sense of humanity to his work that the band felt strongly mirrored their music. It was felt to be inappropriate to copy Wyeth's style by commissioning another artist. Working with the photographer Stefan Ruiz provided the springboard into this world and also placated the record company given that he was the photographer used for Caterpillar. The photography was not to be a literal translation of Wyeth's paintings, rather an opportunity to capture the spirit. The shots were taken within a 50-mile radius of San Francisco using street cast models taking these people to places with the idea of fusing them into the landscapes or interiors. The placement of the image on a White ground is to replicate the way an image is reproduced in an artists monograph, the logo being retained from previous campaigns as it was very much part of the bands identity.

1

| 1 |

TRAVIS"SING" / 7" (Front)   Independiente Ltd   2001   Art Direction: Mark Tappin
Photo: Stefan Ruiz

TRAVIS
SING

1			TRAVIS "MORE THAN US" / EP (Front)	Independiente Ltd	1998	Art Direction: Mark Tappin
						Photo: Bridget Smith
2	1	2	TRAVIS "MORE THAN US" / EP (Inner Gatefold)	Independiente Ltd	1998	Art Direction: Mark Tappin
		3				Photo: Stefan Ruiz
3			TRAVIS "MORE THAN US" / EP (Back)	Independiente Ltd	1998	Art Direction: Mark Tappin
						Photo: Bridget Smith

TRAVIS.
MORE THAN US E.P

1. More than us 2. Give me some truth 3. All I want to do is rock 4. Funny thing

Track 1. Written by F. Healy. Original production by Steve Lillywhite, recorded at Bearsville Studios, NY, engineered by
John Sikel. Strings orchestrated & arranged by Ann Dudley @ Angel Studios, mixed by Mark Wallis @ Metropolis Studios.
Track 2. Written by John Lennon. Produced and mixed by Mark Wallis @ The Townhouse Studios.
Track 3. Written by F. Healy. Live at Manchester 14/12/97, guitars by Noel Gallagher courtesy of Creation Records. Track.
4. Written by F. Healy. Produced and mixed by Tim Simenon, engineered by Ben Hillier @ Mayfair Studios.
All Tracks published by Sony/ATV Music Publishing Ltd, expect Track 2. Published by Northern Songs Ltd.
The copyright in this sound recording is owned by Independiente Ltd. All rights reserved. Unauthorised copying, hiring,
lending, public performance and broadcasting prohibited.
℗1998 Independiente Ltd. ©1998 Independiente Ltd. ℗1998 Independiente Ltd.

TRAVIS.
MORE THAN US E.P

1. More than us (with Ann Dudley)
2. Gimma some truth (by John Lennon)
3. All I want do is rock (with Noel Gallagher)
4. Funny thing (with Tim Simenon)

Independiente   BIEM/MCPS   ISOM 11S

7 24381 16822 6

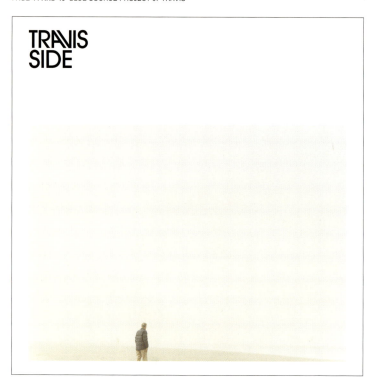

TRAVIS
SIDE

ₐₛSide
ₐₐAll The Young Dudes (Live at Barrowlands)

Track A1 written by F. Healy. Track B1 written by D. Bowie. Track
A1 produced and mixed by Nigel Godrich. Track A1 recorded and
mixed at Ocean Way Studios (L.A). Track B1 recorded at Glasgow
Barrowlands. Mixed by Steve Orchard at Mayfair Studios. Track B1
keyboards by Jeremy Procter. Assistant engineer at Ocean Way Studios
– Darrell Thorp. Track A1 mastered by Bernie Grundman Mastering
(L.A). Track B1 mastered at Metropolis Studios. Track A1 published
by Sony/ATV Music Publishing Ltd. Track B1 published by Chrysalis
Songs/EMI Music Publishing Ltd/Rzo Music c/o Tintoretto Music.
The copyright in this sound recording is owned by Independiente Ltd.
All rights of the manufacturer and of the owner of the recorded work
reserved. Unauthorised copying, hiring, lending, public performance
and broadcasting prohibited. ℗ & © 2001 Independiente Ltd. MCPS.
ISOM 54S. www.independiente.co.uk Art Direction by Blue Source.
Photography by Stefan Ruiz. www.travisonline.com

7 24381 16822 6

1		TRAVIS "SIDE" / 7" (Front)		Independiente Ltd	1999	Art Direction: Mark Tappin Photo: Stefan Ruiz
2		TRAVIS "SIDE" / 7" (Back)		Independiente Ltd	1999	Art Direction: Mark Tappin Photo: Stefan Ruiz
3		TRAVIS "COMING AROUND" / 7" (Front)		Independiente Ltd	2000	Art Direction: Mark Tappin Photo: Bridget Smith
4		TRAVIS "COMING AROUND" / 7" (Back)		Independiente Ltd	2000	Art Direction: Mark Tappin Photo: Bridget Smith

1	2	3	4

01 COMING AROUND
02 THE CONNECTION

PROJECT 08 OTHERS

GLOSS

The creation of the imagery for this campaign was approached as a series of individual works. Blue Source commissioned Julie Verhoeven. Julie was interested to make visual connections with the lyrics and along with blue source created the premise of giving each sleeve a distinctive colour bias. Final artwork utilised the band's logo that would be slowly introduced along the chronology of the campaign's releases. Julie thoroughly developed the concept by producing many pieces of work, which were edited to form the set of campaign sleeves. The project was a perfect example of placing the right individual with the right project and allowing creative freedom to exist within pre-determined parameters.

CATERPILLAR

Caterpillar is the world's largest manufacturer of construction machinery. This heritage has been harnessed to create a classic range of work wear clothing. The values associated with heavy industry have been synthesised to create a robust, functional brand reflecting the rich history of Caterpillar.

Blue Source, using a conceptual framework that lasted for several years, produced an award winning pan-European press campaign. The subject was the modern worker. Photographer Stefan Ruiz was instrumental in the development of a visual style that utilised the language of social documentary, visiting over 10 major cities around the world to document real people at their workplace using CAT work wear.

WINO

As western culture continually seeks to represent typical imagery of Japanese culture, this project sought to explore this process in reverse. The campaign idea was kept very simple; Blue Source conducted a micro photographic study of the humble British garage. This idea was principally motivated by a desire to capture and document, the domestic, suburban locations where thousands of bands have found the refuge to perform and rehearse. Ali Peck is a young photographer who was commissioned for his ability to capture this formal subject in a uniquely British way.

JAMES

For the 'Pleased to Meet You' album cover Blue Source conceived the idea of a presenting the band as a singular James character. Fashion photographer Phil Poynter was commissioned to take portraits of each of the seven band members. From these images a series of low-resolution composites were created using elements from each band member, finally two versions were chosen and presented to the client; a generic everyman version and a second darker more disturbing character who became the basis for the final sleeve image. Basic development and design of the character took place at Blue Source; the final images were constructed in high resolution, using a digital retouching house. In the final package, decoding of this image is aided through the reproduction of all of the original individual portraits. The use of Akzidenz Grotesque was deliberate in rendering its function secondary to the image, attaching itself as a by-line character and statement.

KOSHEEN

Blue Source brief for the Kosheen project was to create an identity relating both to nature, technology and Britishness. Already knowing French photographer, Patrice Hannicote and his work, this project seemed perfect for collaboration. Patrice had been developing a project taking stills of the old museum displays at the Natural History Museum of New York, Blue Source saw this project develop and approached Patrice with the idea of it being published in the form of a set of sleeves for the band. The image of the stag seemed to sum up what the band were visually aiming for it being painterly, classic and British. The functional typography with catalogue numbering beneath the title serves as a signifier of how artefacts are documented and catalogued whilst juxtaposing the images organic, naturalistic quality.

GLOSS
LONELY
IN
PARIS

1				GLOSS "NEW YORK BOY" / 7"	Nude Records	2001	Design: Mark Tappin Cover Art: Julie Verhoeven
	1	2	3				
2				GLOSS "THIS IS ALL I NEED" / 7"	Nude Records	2001	Design: Mark Tappin Cover Art: Julie Verhoeven
3				GLOSS "MY HEART BELONGS TO YOU" / 7"	Nude Records	2001	Design: Mark Tappin Cover Art: Julie Verhoeven

NEW ZEALANDER IN ODAIBA
PROOFED MICRO-FIBRE HOODED JACKET
+44 20 7860 0131

AMERICAN IN ICHIGAYA
GIRLS DUFFEL COAT
+44 (0) 20 7860 0131

PAGE 50 and 51

1		
2	1	2

CATERPILLAR APPAREL PAN-EUROPEAN ADVERTISING CAMPAIGN A/W 99 / Press Ad Execution 15   Caterpillar   1999   Art Direction: Leigh Marling
Design: Simon Gofton
Photo: Stefan Ruiz

CATERPILLAR APPAREL PAN-EUROPEAN ADVERTISING CAMPAIGN A/W 99 / Press Ad Execution 29   Caterpillar   1999   Art Direction: Leigh Marling
Design: Simon Gofton
Photo: Stefan Ruiz

1		
2	1	2

CATERPILLAR APPAREL PAN-EUROPEAN ADVERTISING CAMPAIGN A/W 99 / Press Ad Execution 7   Caterpillar   1999   Art Direction: Leigh Marling
Design: Simon Gofton
Photo: Stefan Ruiz

CATERPILLAR APPAREL PAN-EUROPEAN ADVERTISING CAMPAIGN A/W 99 / Press Ad Execution 8   Caterpillar   1999   Art Direction: Leigh Marling
Design: Simon Gofton
Photo: Stefan Ruiz

1			WINO"EVERLAST" / CD Album (Front)		Victor Entertainment Inc	2002	Design: Simon Parkinson
	1	2					Photo: Ali Peck
2			WINO "LOVE IS HERE" / CD Single (Front)		Victor Entertainment Inc	2002	Design: Simon Parkinson
							Photo: Ali Peck

James
Pleased To Meet You

1			JAMES "PLEASED TO MEET YOU" / CD Album (Front)	Mercury Records Ltd	2001	Design: Simon Earith Photo: Phil Poynter
	1	2				
2			JAMES "GETTING AWAY WITH IT" (ALL MESSED UP) / CD Single (Front)	Mercury Records Ltd	2001	Design: Simon Earith Photo: Phil Poynter

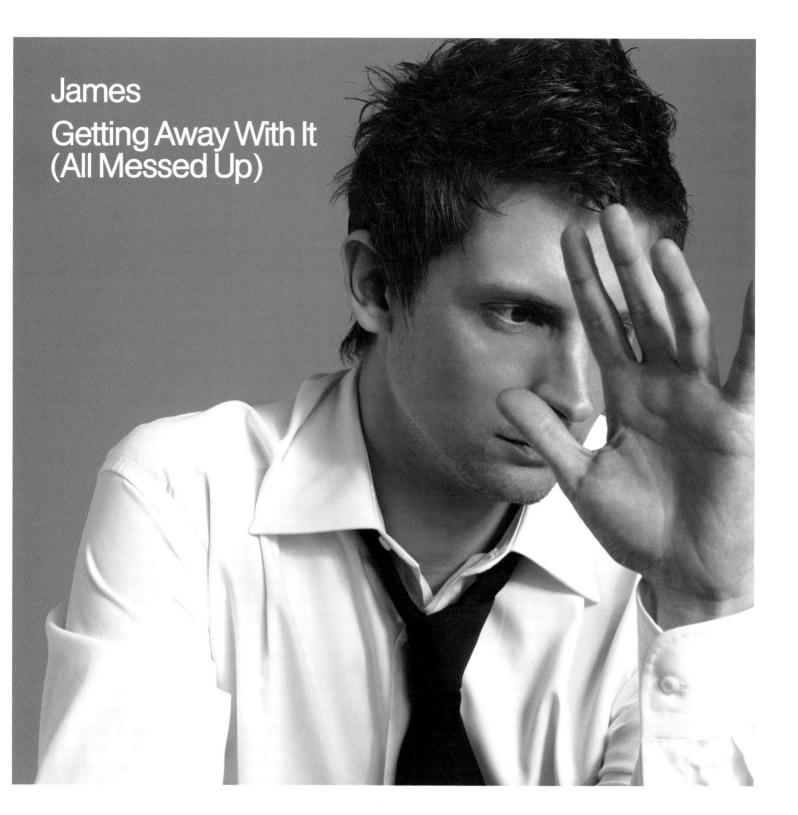

James
Getting Away With It
(All Messed Up)

KOSHEEN:RESIST
74321880812

1			KOSHEEN "RESIST" / CD Album (Front)	Arista / BMG	2001	Design: Simon Earith Photo: Patrice Hanicotte
2	1	2	KOSHEEN "HUNGRY" / CD Single (Front)	Arista / BMG	2001	Design: Simon Earith Photo: Patrice Hanicotte

KOSHEEN:HUNGRY
74321934382

KOSHEEN:HARDER
74321954452

1			KOSHEEN "HARDER" / CD Single (Front)	Arista / BMG	2002	Design: Simon Earith Photo: Patrice Hanicotte
1	1	2	KOSHEEN "HIDEU" / CD Single (Front)	Arista / BMG	2001	Design: Simon Earith Photo: Patrice Hanicotte

KOSHEEN:HIDEU
74321878962

Blue Source
ANSWERS

TEL
FAX
ISDN
e-mail
www.bluesource.com

in its absence
_____
1) When you most feel the presence of 'design' around you?

parallelogram (high scrabble score)
_____
2) What is your favorite shape?

yesterday, today + tomorrow
_____
3) What was your happiest moment in your work experience?

RGB
_____
4) Please list up your 3 favorite colors

I hate hate, but don't you know I love love.
_____
5) What do you hate the most?

lycra balsawood + perspex
_____
6) Please list up your 3 favorite materials.

bed
_____
7) Where is your most favorite place?

buckminster fuller, verner panton, jon maeda
_____
8) Please list up your 3 favorite designers.

make do + mend
_____
9) Please define the word 'design'

okay, yes + maybe
_____
10) Please list up your 3 favorite words.

EDITORIAL
CREDIT

GASBOOK 08
BLUE SOURCE

COVER DESIGN BLUE SOURCE

EDITORIAL DIRECTOR Toru Hachiga
CONTRIBUTING EDITOR & TEXT Daniel Mason
ART DIRECTOR Hideki Inaba
DESIGNER Takanobu Niizeki, Tadamune Yamagata
COORDINATOR Ayako Terashima

EXECUTIVE PRODUCER Takeyuki Fujii
PRODUCER Akira Natsume

PUBLISHER Masanori Omae

Image ©BLUE SOURCE 2002
©2002 DesignEXchange Co.,Ltd.

Published in Japan in 2002 and distributed worldwide by DesignEXchange Co.,Ltd.
Nakameguro GS Dai2 Bldg 2-9-35 Kamimeguro Meguro-ku Tokyo 153-0051 Japan
Phone 81 3 5704 7350   Fax 81 3 5704 7351
e-mail pggas@dex.ne.jp
http://www.dex.ne.jp

ISBN 4-86083-268-X

Printed in Japan by Toppan Printing Co.,Ltd.

First Printing, 2002

PAGE 62 and 63

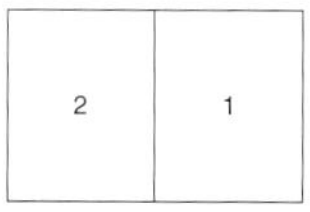

1		BLUE SOURCE OFFICE
2	2	1	QUESTION

PHOTO James Harris